JUN   2012

EDGE BOOKS™

THE GHOST FILES

The World's Most
HAUNTED PLACES

by Matt Chandler

Consultant:
Dr. Andrew Nichols
Director
American Institute of Parapsychology
Gainesville, Florida

CAPSTONE PRESS
a capstone imprint

Edge Books are published by Capstone Press,
1710 Roe Crest Drive, North Mankato, Minnesota 56003.
www.capstonepub.com

Books published by Capstone Press are manufactured with paper
containing at least 10 percent post-consumer waste.

Library of Congress Cataloging-in-Publication Data
Chandler, Matt.
    The world's most haunted places / by Matt Chandler.
    p. cm.—(Edge Books. The Ghost Files)
    Includes bibliographical references and index.
    Summary: "Describes paranormal activity at haunted locations, and relates
stories of places where such activity has been reported"—Provided by publisher.
    ISBN 978-1-4296-6518-6 (library binding)
    1. Haunted places—Juvenile literature. I. Title. II. Series.
BF1461.C43 2012
133.1—dc2   22011003790

Editorial Credits
Aaron Sautter, editor; Tracy Davies, designer; Svetlana Zhurkin,
        media researcher; Eric Manske, production specialist

Photo Credits
Alamy: Dale O'Dell, 6, Edith Dorsey Raff, 5, The Marsden Archive,
17; Courtesy Estes Park Museum, 9; Courtesy The Queen Mary, 21
(both); Darren Vallance, 11, 13; Denise Espino, 26; Dreamstime: Kenk,
24, Konstantin Androsov, 29, Markstout, 7 (bottom); DVIC: NARA, 25;
Getty Images: Hulton Archive, 16, Paul Hawthorne, 15, Popperfoto, 19;
iStockphoto: Albert Kerstna, cover, Katrin Solansky, 18; Library of
Congress, 27; Newscom: Album, 23 (inset); Shutterstock: George
Koroneos, 7 (top), Manamana, 23 (bottom), Yossi Manor, 22

Printed in the United States of America in Stevens Point, Wisconsin.

122011   006527WZVMI

TABLE OF CONTENTS

CHAPTER 1

A CHILLING EXPERIENCE

You turn off the TV on your way out the door. As you step outside, a bolt of lightning streaks through the dark sky. Thunder rumbles as the first drops of rain begin to fall. You decide you need your jacket. When you walk back inside, you discover the TV is on. But you had just turned it off. No one else is home. Who could have turned it on? Could this be the work of a ghost? Is the house haunted?

Nobody really knows if ghosts are real. Some ghost hunters and paranormal researchers say they are. But skeptics don't think the evidence researchers collect proves anything. They say most ghostly events have natural explanations.

paranormal — having to do with unexplained events

However, many strange happenings have not been explained. Locations said to be haunted often see a wide variety of ghostly activities. Strange noises, temperature changes, moving objects, and ghostly figures have all been observed in many places. Read on to learn about some of the world's spookiest places—then decide for yourself if hauntings are fact or fiction.

Did a ghost turn on the TV, or was it simply affected by the storm?

skeptic — someone who questions things other people believe

CHAPTER 2

GHOSTLY FIGURES

Imagine walking down a long, dark hallway. You see a figure approach. Suddenly, you find that you can see right through its body. Just as fear grips you, the ghostly figure disappears. Scary encounters like this are reported every year across the world. Apparitions have been reported everywhere from famous locations like the White House to places like small-town hotels and restaurants.

A Haunted Hotel

Stephen King is a famous author of many horror stories. One of his earliest books was *The Shining*. In the story, a family works as winter caretakers of a large, empty hotel. But the family doesn't know the hotel is full of evil spirits. The spirits drive the father insane, and he tries to kill his family. King was inspired to write the story after staying at the Stanley Hotel in Estes Park, Colorado.

STEPHEN KING

Stanley Hotel, Estes Park, Colorado

There have been many ghost sightings at the Stanley Hotel. People have reported seeing the hotel's former owner, F. O. Stanley, wandering the halls long after he died. Stanley's ghost has often been reported in the billiard room, which was his favorite spot. He doesn't speak or try to visit with hotel guests. But many are frightened when they see his transparent ghost float by.

There have also been reports of mysterious music coming from the hotel ballroom. People have even seen keys on the piano moving on their own. Does a piano-playing ghost haunt the Stanley Hotel too? Some people believe so. But perhaps it is simply people's imaginations running wild after reading King's book.

> **FACT** Lewlawala, an American Indian woman, jumped to her death at Niagara Falls long ago. Each year, people report seeing her ghost floating in the mist high above the falls.

The spirit of F. O. Stanley is said to haunt several parts of his old hotel.

CHAPTER 3

UNEXPLAINED NOISES

Seeing a transparent ghost can be a terrifying experience. But hearing a blood-curdling scream can send shivers down your spine. Several people say they've heard strange noises and voices where many people have died.

SCREAMS FROM THE DEAD

The Waverly Hills Sanatorium was a hospital built in Louisville, Kentucky, in 1926. Tuberculosis (TB) patients were treated there. TB is a deadly disease that attacks a person's lungs, leaving its victims unable to breathe.

Before an effective treatment was found for TB, thousands of people died at Waverly. Doctors didn't want to scare patients by continually wheeling dead bodies past their rooms. Instead, they transported the dead out through a long tunnel. So many bodies went through the tunnel that it became known as the "body chute" or "death tunnel."

Each year, hundreds of dead bodies were sent through Waverly's "death tunnel."

Waverly was changed into a hospital for the elderly in the 1960s. But patients were treated poorly there for many years. Waverly was closed for good in 1981. But it seems that the spirits of some people have never left. Visitors say you can still hear disembodied voices echoing through Waverly's empty halls. Many people have claimed to hear a mysterious voice yelling, "Get out!"

Some people have also reported seeing the ghost of an old woman. She is bound in chains, and blood drips down her arms as she runs from the building. Witnesses say she screams, "Help me, somebody save me!" as she flees.

FACT In the 1800s a spirit known as the Bell Witch supposedly terrified the Bell family in Tennessee. The haunting began with strange scratching sounds during the night. When John Bell died, several family members believed the witch poisoned him.

disembodied — when a person's spirit is separated from the body

Waverly Hills Sanatorium

CHAPTER 4

EXTREME TEMPERATURES

Many haunted locations have one thing in common. Witnesses claim that the temperature quickly changes. One corner of a room might suddenly become freezing cold. Meanwhile, other spots feel incredibly hot. Some people believe this phenomenon is evidence of ghostly activity.

HOT AND COLD

In 1974 Ronald DeFeo Jr. murdered his parents and siblings in their home in Amityville, New York. George and Kathy Lutz bought the house in 1975. But they were not prepared for the terrifying experiences they were about to have.

phenomenon — something very unusual or remarkable

As soon as the Lutzes moved in, they began hearing strange noises. They also experienced other odd things. One day the temperature began to rise. It was January, and the temperature outside was just 20 degrees Fahrenheit (minus 7 degrees Celsius). A storm had knocked out the power and heat. But inside the house, the temperature continued to rise. At one point it reached 90°F (32°C).

The Lutz family was terrified by the many strange events at their house in Amityville.

George Lutz had the opposite experience with temperatures. From their first night in the house, he said he felt chilled to the bone. The thermostat said it was 80°F (27°C), but he felt freezing cold.

What was causing the temperature changes? Was it the spirits of the murdered family tormenting the Lutz family? For the Lutzes, it finally became too much to handle. They only lived in their new home for 28 days. They fled the house fearing for their lives and never returned.

George and Kathy Lutz

FACT There were widespread reports that the Amityville haunting was a hoax. But George and Kathy Lutz both passed lie detector tests. They claimed their story was true until they died.

HAUNTED OR HOAX?

The Borley Rectory in Essex, England, was once known as the most haunted house in the country. Families and visitors to the house between 1928 and 1937 reported many paranormal activities. It burned down in 1939.

Researchers later investigated the Borley Rectory and the claims of ghosts haunting the building. No explanation was ever found for the strange activity there.

But more than 50 years later, Louis Mayerling published a book claiming that the Borley ghosts were a hoax. Mayerling said he had known the original owner, Reverend Bull. Mayerling claimed that the Reverend and others enjoyed pretending that the building was haunted to scare guests. However, it was later revealed that Mayerling had made up his claims. Did restless spirits haunt the Borley Rectory? Perhaps the world will never know.

CHAPTER 5

MOVING OBJECTS

Sometimes strange, unexplained activity can be just as creepy as seeing a ghost. Lights might turn themselves on and off. Doors and windows may open and close on their own. Perhaps objects fly across the room. Whatever form it takes, this strange activity can be enough to send people running in terror.

THE GHOST SHIP

The *Queen Mary* was a famous passenger ship in the 1930s. It could carry up to 3,000 people. At the beginning of World War II (1939–1945), the ship was painted gray and given the nickname the "Gray Ghost." It became a warship and was used to transport soldiers.

Many soldiers and crew members died serving on the ship during the war. In 1967 the ship was moved to Long Beach, California, and turned into a floating hotel. Since then, guests on the *Queen Mary* regularly report many strange activities.

The Queen Mary transported thousands of soldiers during World War II.

One report involves the ship's cook, who was murdered on board during the war. Today many strange events have been seen in the ship's kitchen. Witnesses say pots and pans move by themselves and sometimes disappear. Doors open and close on their own. And rattling and banging sounds can be heard. Could it be the ghost of the cook?

The cook's ghost may not be alone. Guests have also reported strange events in their bedrooms. Blankets are mysteriously ripped off beds as the guests are sleeping. The lights turn on by themselves. People jump from their beds, screaming and terrified—only to find that no one is there.

These strange events could be proof that the *Queen Mary* is haunted. But they could also simply be the result of people's active imaginations. Nobody knows for certain.

FACT

At least two men were crushed to death by a watertight door on the *Queen Mary*. The dead men are said to haunt the ship's engine room where they were killed.

Strange activity is often reported in the Queen Mary's kitchens.

Visitors often report ghostly activities in some of the ship's guest rooms.

CHAPTER 6

MYSTERIOUS MUSIC

Some ghost hunters think ghosts might use music to communicate from beyond the grave. Witnesses claim they've heard pianos playing themselves and guitars strumming in empty rooms.

CAPONE'S BANJO

One place known for haunting music is the old prison on Alcatraz Island in San Francisco, California. For more than 100 years, some of America's most dangerous criminals were kept there. Alcatraz closed its doors in 1963. Since then, there have been several reports of ghosts haunting the old prison.

Perhaps the most infamous criminal ever locked up at Alcatraz was Al Capone. Capone was a Chicago gangster who was imprisoned for not paying taxes. The crime boss was known for playing a banjo while in prison. Today visitors sometimes report hearing banjo music in the prison's shower room. Is it the ghost of Capone? Nobody knows.

AL CAPONE

Alcatraz prison held some of history's most infamous criminals.

FACT Al Capone's banjo was a gift from his wife. He played in a prison band along with gangster George Kelly Barnes. Best known as "Machine Gun Kelly," Barnes played drums in the band.

REPEATING THE PAST

Many locations are said to be haunted by people who once lived or worked there. In some cases, people report seeing spirits repeating activities they performed while alive. Handymen who were murdered in hotels appear to fix toilets. Dead chefs are seen in kitchens preparing meals. And soldiers killed in battle are seen patrolling old battlefields.

Caught in Time

In early July 1863, one of the bloodiest battles of the Civil War (1861–1865) took place at Gettysburg, Pennsylvania. Tens of thousands of soldiers were killed in the fighting. Many of the dead were left to rot in the fields where they fell. It's no surprise that Gettysburg is reportedly one of the most haunted places in the United States.

After the battle, the fields near Gettysburg were filled with thousands of dead soldiers.

Today visitors to Gettysburg often report seeing the misty spirits of soldiers lined up on the battlefields. They appear to be getting ready for a bloody fight. There have also been sightings at Gettysburg College. During the battle, the Confederate Army took over Pennsylvania Hall. It was used as a hospital for wounded Confederate soldiers. Students have reported seeing soldiers' spirits still guarding their posts.

Some investigators say the suffering at horrific battles such as Gettysburg can leave a psychic imprint on the land. That imprint is often replayed, and it can last for hundreds of years.

Photos showing ghostly orbs have been taken on Little Round Top hill near Gettysburg.

Many ghostly activities have been reported at Gettysburg College.

GHOSTS:
FACT OR FANTASY?

Are ghosts and other paranormal activity real? Or are there obvious explanations for the strange things people hear and see? No one can be certain either way. Many stories of haunted places are easily proven false. Others are more difficult to explain.

The next time you hear something strange and a shiver runs down your spine, you might wonder if it's a ghost. But it's more likely to be something perfectly ordinary, such as the wind blowing outside. Even so, it can be fun to wonder if ghosts and haunted places might be real.

FACT The Banff Springs Hotel in Canada reportedly has a famous bellman named Sam. He offers to carry guests' bags and helps those who are locked out of their rooms. There's just one problem—Sam died in 1976!

GLOSSARY

apparition (ap-uh-RISH-uhn)—the visible appearance of a ghost

disembodied (dis-em-BOD-eed)—when a person's soul is separated from the body

hoax (HOHKS)—a trick to make people believe something that is not true

insane (in-SAYN)—mentally ill

paranormal (par-uh-NOHR-muhl)—having to do with an unexplained event that has no scientific explanation

phenomenon (fe-NOM-uh-non)—something very unusual or remarkable

psychic (SYE-kik)—having to do with a person's soul or mind

skeptic (SKEP-tik)—a person who questions things that other people believe in

transparent (trans-PAIR-uhnt)—easily seen through

READ MORE

Axelrod-Contrada, Joan. *Ghoulish Ghost Stories.* Scary Stories. Mankato, Minn.: Capstone Press, 2011.

Parvis, Sarah. *Haunted Hotels.* Scary Places. New York: Bearport Publishing, 2008.

Williams, Dinah. *Haunted Houses.* Scary Places. New York: Bearport Publishing, 2008.

INTERNET SITES

FactHound offers a safe, fun way to find Internet sites related to this book. All of the sites on FactHound have been researched by our staff.

Here's all you do:

Visit *www.facthound.com*

Type in this code: 9781429665186

INDEX